Voyager Missions!
Where Are They Now and What They Have Discovered!

Space Science for Kids

Children's Astrophysics & Space Science Books

All Rights reserved. No part of this book may be reproduced or used in any way or form or by any means whether electronic or mechanical, this means that you cannot record or photocopy any material ideas or tips that are provided in this book.

Copyright 2016

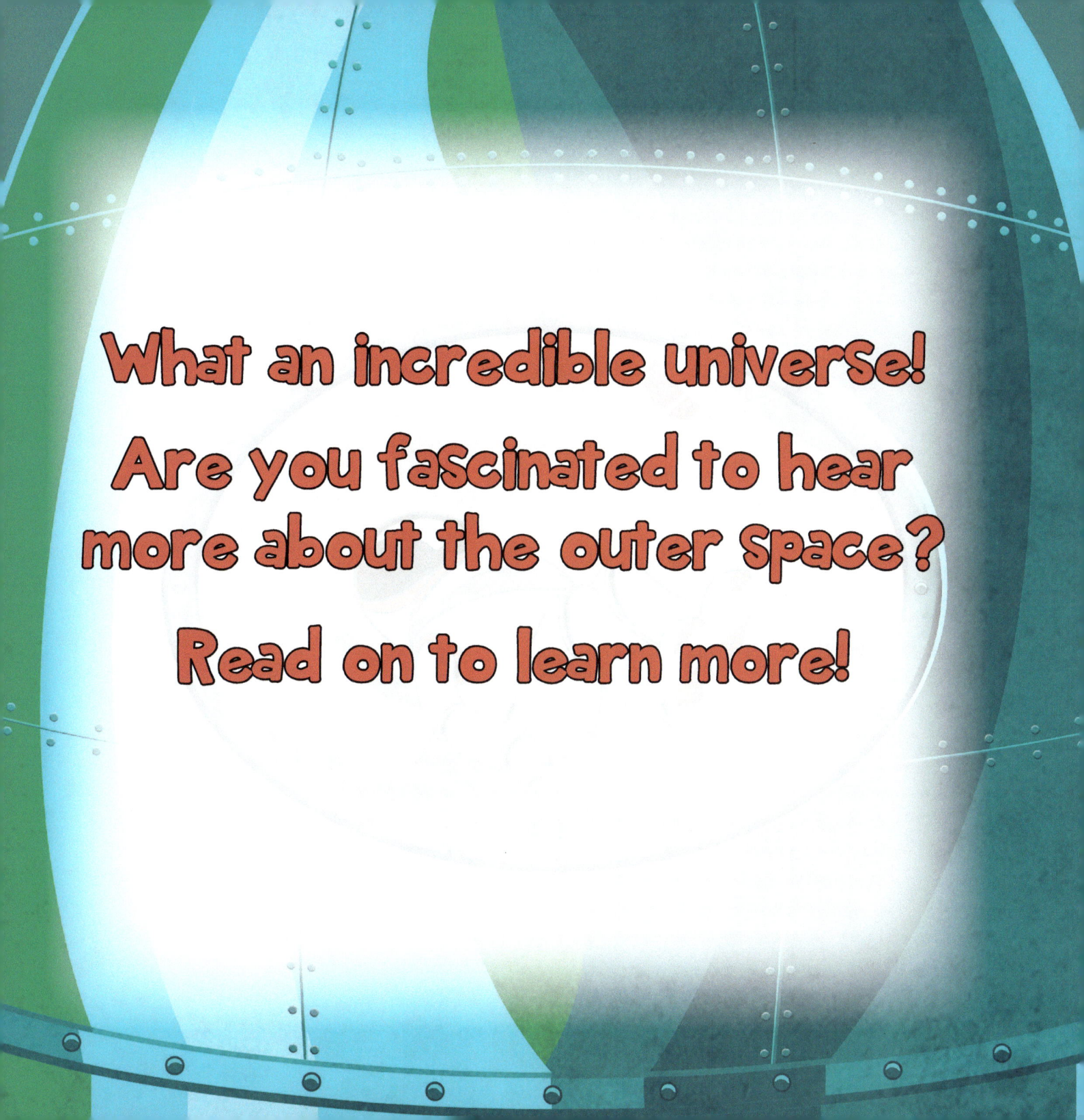

What an incredible universe!

Are you fascinated to hear more about the outer space?

Read on to learn more!

The Voyager missions discovered the existence of the outer planets.

Because of these missions, you are able to see these planets and study them, too.

In 1977, the Voyager 1 Spacecraft was launched from the Kennedy Space Center.

Its mission was to explore, observe and gather data about the atmospheres, interiors, satellites and magnetospheres of Jupiter and Saturn.

Its cameras recorded 32,000 pictures of Jupiter's and Saturn's moons and rings.

As part of its mission, it also took 60 pictures of the Solar System: the sun and the six planets.

Its final task, before its cameras were turned off, was to take pictures of the Sun, Venus, Earth, Jupiter, Saturn, Uranus and Neptune.

Voyager 2 spacecraft was launched on August 20, 1977 with the mission of exploring all the outer planets and their satellites.

Voyager 2 left the Earth before Voyager 1 but arrived at Jupiter four months behind Voyager 1.

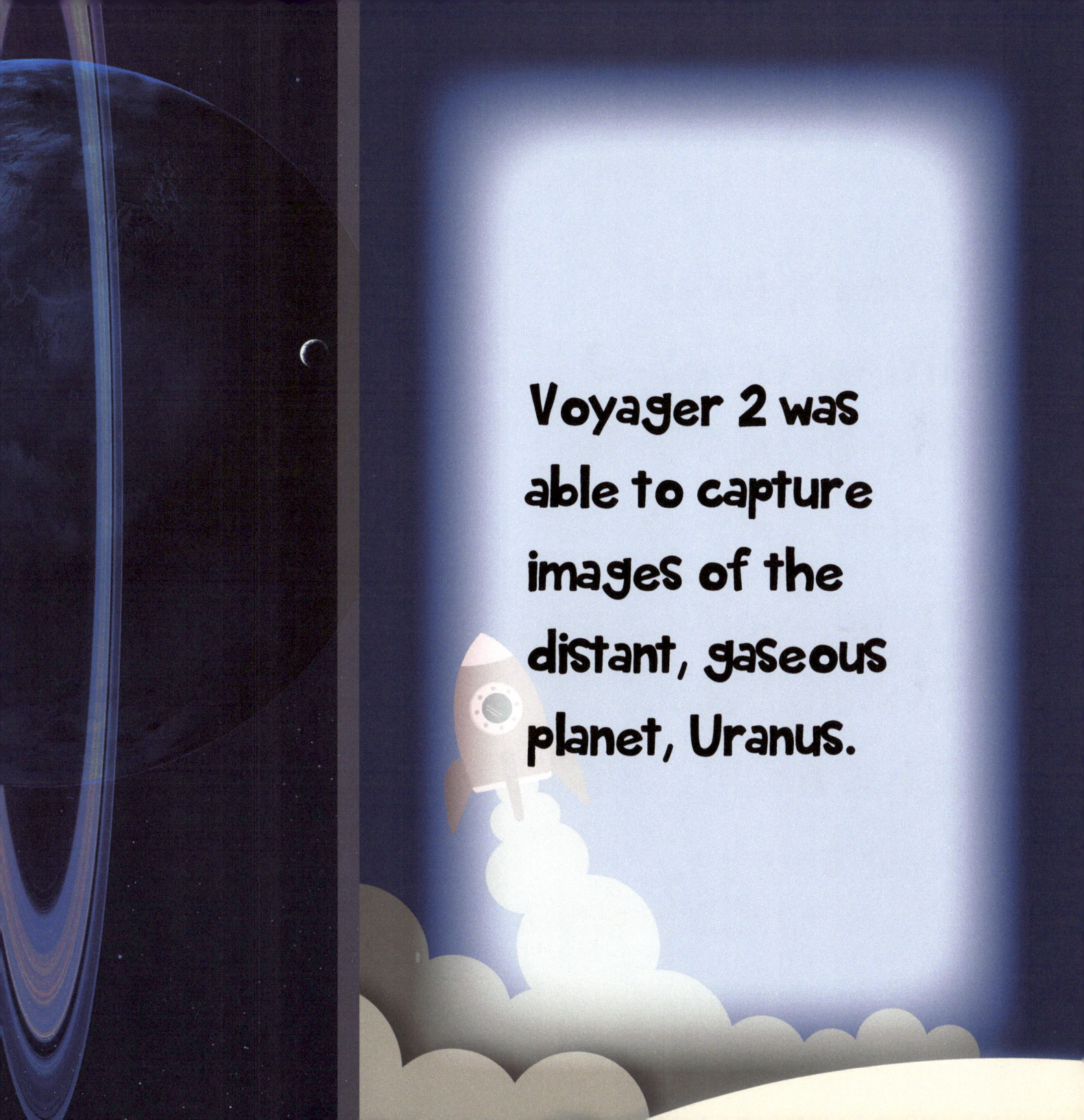

Voyager 2 was able to capture images of the distant, gaseous planet, Uranus.

The captured images revealed that Uranus is the coldest planet in the Solar System because it has no internal heat source.

Voyager 2 also discovered 10 new moons and two new rings around Uranus.

In August 1989, Voyager 2 arrived in Neptune and captured 10,000 images.

One of its images showed that there was a Great Dark Spot in Neptune like the Great Red Spot in Jupiter, which was considered as an atmospheric hole like the one in the Earth's ozone layer.

After 37 years in outer space, NASA's Voyager 1 and Voyager 2 spacecrafts are still very functional.

Can you imagine how sturdy they are to have withstood space for such a very long time?

Let's keep track on Voyager's Interstellar Space Missions to learn more about the universe!

www.ingramcontent.com/pod-product-compliance
Lightning Source LLC
Chambersburg PA
CBHW041226040426
42444CB00002B/61